William & Sam Go to the Farm

First published 2022
Copyright © Anna Zarb 2022

The right of Anna Zarb to be identified as the author of this work has been asserted in accordance with the Copyright, Designs & Patents Act 1988.

All rights reserved. No part of this book may be reproduced, stored in a retrieval system, or transmitted in any form or by any means, electronic, electrostatic, magnetic tape, mechanical, photocopying, recording or otherwise, without the written permission of the copyright holder.

Published under licence by Brown Dog Books and
The Self-Publishing Partnership Ltd, 10b Greenway Farm, Bath Rd, Wick, nr. Bath BS30 5RL

www.selfpublishingpartnership.co.uk

ISBN printed book: 978-1-83952-461-5
ISBN e-book: 978-1-83952-462-2

Cover and internal design by Andrew Prescott
Illustrated by Sophia Hammett

Printed and bound in the UK
This book is printed on FSC certified paper

MIX
Paper from responsible sources
FSC® C013604
FSC www.fsc.org

The Adventures of William & Sam

William & Sam Go to the Farm

Anna Zarb
Illustrated by Sophia Hammett

BROWN DOG BOOKS

Dedicated to my beautiful mother.

Chapter one

William was running full pelt after the chicken. Stones and dirt were flicking up behind him, thrown into the air by the force of his paws pushing off the ground. He HAD to catch this chicken. Catching the chicken was even more important than William's afternoon nap. Hearing the commotion behind her, the chicken turned her head slightly to the side to help her focus, only to see a vicious-looking dog running straight at her. Her eyes bulged and she panicked, squawked and flapped her wings. She ran away from William as fast as she could with her neck stretched forward and her body rocking from side to side like a wobbling weeble. Unfortunately, she ran straight out of the farm gate onto the long driveway.

"Wait, come back!" William yelled after her, but the chicken was not stopping for anything. Chickens can be easily scared, and it seemed this one was no exception. William needed to get to her before she reached the lane. Luckily, Jimmy the farm dog woke from his nap, and on hearing the mayhem he ran outside to investigate.

"William tried to chase the chicken back in, but it ran even further away," explained Sam, William's sister, as fast as she could, the words tumbling out of her mouth. Jimmy sprang into action and ran out of the gate and down the driveway faster than when Lewis and his sister Millie run when they hear the jingle of the ice-cream van.

"Out of my way," he shouted to William as he sprinted past, his ears were being forced back by the wind and his tail was straight out behind him. He stretched his front legs as far as they would go in front of him and his back legs were stretched out behind, all four legs were off the ground as if he were flying through the air. He was definitely going to save that chicken. He overtook the chicken, screeched to a halt and turned around all at once. The chicken, now faced with an even bigger, scarier dog, squawked, turned back and ran down the driveway. Jimmy followed her to make sure she got safely back through the farm gate. As the chicken approached William, William dived into the hedge to get out of her way, he did not want her turning back round again on seeing him. He waited for Jimmy to go past and then trudged back to the farm gate. He went much more slowly now, his ears were low and his head was down, an air of melancholy surrounded him. He did not want to have to face Jimmy. He hated being told off almost as much as he hated being brushed.

"I was only trying to help," William said defensively as he came back through the gate. He wanted to get his explanation in first as he was worried that Jimmy was going to shout at him.

"You're not supposed to run at them," Jimmy scowled at him. Jimmy's one green eye and one blue eye made him look even more forbidding. "You scared her. You have to sneak past, giving them a wide berth so as not to frighten them, and then herd them back in when you've passed them so they are at least heading in the right direction." William did not believe the incident to be his fault though, after all, Jimmy had not explained that before. He had just said that if a chicken escapes, then to chase her back in, and that's exactly what William had tried to do. Jimmy then barked to let the farmers, Fred and Molly, know the gate was open. Molly marched round the corner.

"Good boy, Jimmy," she said as she came over to shut the gate. "I expect an egg customer left it open. Hope you lot are having fun together," she said to the dogs as they were all sitting together. Jimmy gave a withering sigh and went back into the farmhouse kitchen leaving the other two by the gate. He really didn't need the bother of these two amateur dogs coming onto his farm and scaring the animals. He worked hard to protect them and keep them safe; this was going to be a long day.

William was still trembling from his encounter with Jimmy. His bid to become a farm dog had not started well, but he still had the rest of the day to impress Jimmy. He just had to figure out how. He did not know that he wanted to be a farm dog until they had arrived at the farm earlier that morning, in fact he didn't know that dogs actually had jobs at all. He and Sam filled their days with playing, going for walks and getting attention from their human family. When he realised he could be in charge of other animals, he started imagining himself as a working dog, his stature rose as he felt himself becoming full of importance and he puffed out his chest. He could be top dog. He decided at that point that if he worked hard today then maybe, just maybe, he would be allowed to work there. This dream however had already started to fade away; he had been at the farm less than an hour and he was already in Jimmy's bad books.

William could, of course, start by following the instructions that Jimmy had given them when they had arrived at the farm. Jimmy had specifically told them not to get too close to the animals, especially the horses as they had metal shoes on. If they got too close then they might get stood on, or even worse, scare them. William had certainly succeeded in the latter. William and Sam had arrived at the farm with their human family for Lewis's twelfth birthday. Jimmy had not been too impressed at their arrival and gave them a job that they could do. This job was twofold. They had to sit by the gate and bark, firstly to alert the farmers if anybody came in and left the gate open, and secondly to keep an eye out for any chicken escapees. But William suggested to his sister Sam that they went exploring instead. His eyes had lit up with excitement at the thought of exploring the large farm, Sam on the other hand liked to follow the rules, the muscles in her face had twitched, she was worried about that plan. She knew the farm dog Jimmy was not a dog to get into trouble with. It turned out that she was right.

"Well, that went well," Sam rolled her eyes.

"Let's go and find Lewis and Millie." William wanted some comfort after the drama. They stumbled across the chicken coop first.

"No running," Sam instructed. There was room inside the coop for quite a few chickens as they are social animals so like to be with each other. There were perches up high for the chickens to sleep safely and lots of room for them to move around. However, there was not a chicken to be seen inside as they had been let out for the day. They are shut in at night to keep them secure from foxes. Foxes are cunning predators that come out at night-time and enjoy a chicken or two for dinner if they are not locked away safely. In the coop William and Sam sniffed the air, there was a strange aroma to the barn; they had not been in a chicken's house before. They bumped into Lewis and Millie, the children in their human family.

"Hi William, hi Sam, I hope you're enjoying being at the farm so far. It's fun isn't it?" Millie's wide smile and gleaming teeth showed how excited she was to be there. Even though the visit was for Lewis's birthday, Millie was having a great time learning about the different animals too. Molly was showing them how to clean the coop and handed Lewis a brush. "It's really important that the animals are properly looked after and we show them compassion."

Molly continued to speak to the children.

> *"For an animal to have a high standard of welfare,*
> *They must have the very best of care.*
> *For an animal to be healthy and happy,*
> *They must not live anywhere unnatural or shabby.*
> *To provide an animal with what it needs,*
> *You must know about the different species and breeds.*
> *So, to stop any animals coming to harm,*
> *You must make the very best conditions on the farm."*

Lewis and Millie understood and got to work cleaning out the coop until it was nice and clean for the chickens. The next task was to check for eggs.

"I wonder what they're doing. Why are they carrying buckets?" William whispered to Sam. Lewis and Millie were collecting the eggs from the nest boxes. These are safe places where the chickens can lay their eggs. The children placed the eggs as carefully as possible onto straw at the base of the buckets. The straw made a nice soft place for the eggs to stay before being put into egg boxes to be sold. Eggs are very fragile and can be broken easily so they have to be handled with extreme care.

"Looks like they are collecting eggs, they eat them for breakfast sometimes," Sam explained.

"Oh," said William and decided that if Lewis and Millie ate them, then they must be nice. He then sniffed around the coop, his nose skimming the ground until he came across an egg. Luckily for him one of the chickens had not used a nest box.

"Found one," he yelled to Sam. He opened his jaw wide and put his teeth around the egg. He gave an almighty bite, not realising how delicate egg shells are. The shell cracked and the egg exploded in his face. Egg white and yolk were dripping from his teeth and nose, it was all gooey and sticky.

"Urgh, that's horrible," cried William and spat out bits of egg shell and raw egg.

"You're not supposed to eat it like that," laughed Sam, "Mum cooks them in a pan first."

"You could have told me that before, my beard's all sticky now." William sulked. He tried to wipe the raw egg off his face by rubbing his face on the ground. This just resulted in making his beard even more grubby as the dirt stuck to the sticky egg. Now his lovely white beard was a dull, horrid brown.

Fred strolled into the barn to see how Lewis and Millie were getting on. He saw the broken egg on the floor.

"Do be careful children, we sell these eggs and need them all intact."

"Sorry," Millie said. "It must have rolled onto the floor without us noticing. We have been extremely careful not to break any." Her cheeks flushed pink.

Fred was not angry; accidents happen sometimes.

"That's okay; just try not to break any more." Fred winked then checked the buckets to make sure the rest of the eggs were in one piece. They were, so he left them to it.

"I can't believe you broke an egg," huffed Lewis, annoyed that they could have gotten into trouble.

"I didn't," objected Millie. "It must have rolled onto the floor and broken just like I said." She could tell Lewis did not really believe her, she didn't know what else to say to persuade him that it wasn't her fault. She felt very sorry for herself and her eyes filled with tears.

"Come on Sam, let's go," William said. Sam had really wanted to stay and comfort Millie but William decided that it was best if they left the chicken coop as quickly as possible and found somewhere else to go to avoid any more 'accidents'. William never meant to get anybody, or himself, into trouble. He just seemed to attract it. As they sped outside, some of the chickens were there, pecking and scratching the ground. Chickens love to search for food and are excellent at detecting motion, which helps them to find lots of insects and bugs to eat. Fred was refilling the water drinkers and feeders.

"Hello there dogs," he greeted them with a stroke. His huge hands were as big as shovels. They were rough and cracked, signs of how hard he worked, and they felt so gigantic against their bodies. Despite his size, he was very gentle. Fred's bright, glittering blue eyes were shining and the mischief in them almost matched the mischief in William's eyes. The wrinkles around Fred's eyes creased as he smiled at them, the deep lines reminded William of dental sticks and he gave him a big lick. Fred screwed up his face and laughed.

"I've been told that you will be on your best behaviour today." Mum and dad were friends with Fred and Molly, and Fred and Molly were delighted to have the family at the farm for the day and teach the children about animals. They were happy for the dogs to come too as long as they behaved. Mum and Dad had made a faithful promise that William and Sam would be on their best behaviour and all the animals will be safe. They were yet to realise that their promise had already been broken.

Molly came over and knelt beside Fred. The sun caught her beautiful auburn hair and it shimmered in the light, her dancing green eyes lit with kindness. She gently stroked the dogs under the chin; this is better than patting the top of their heads, which can be unnerving for dogs. As her hair cascaded down, it looked like a cord on one of William's tug toys. He fought the urge to grab it between his teeth and give it a good shake with all his might. Her cheeks were so smooth, like the jelly on his dog food, so he gave her a good lick instead.

"Ah, thank you William, aren't you so cute," she cooed. It appeared William had won over both Molly and Fred, now he just needed to work on Jimmy.

William, pleased with himself, turned his attention back to the chickens. One chicken was moving slightly differently from the others. Her feathers were all fluffed up, she was moving the loose soil beneath her with her beak. She then lay down in the bowl she had created and lifted her feathers.

"What are you doing?" asked William, amused at the way she was moving.

She replied, "Having a dust bath."

"Dust bathing is one of our favourite things,
We kick up the dust and spread it over our wings.
Getting rid of old oils and parasites is our mission,
This keeps our feathers in tip-top condition."

The chicken spent a little while doing this. Once she was finished, she stood up then wriggled and jiggled, shaking herself to get rid of the loose soil.

"That's better," she squawked, feeling very satisfied.

William thought that looked very pleasurable so he got in her spot and rolled onto his back rubbing it deep into the soil.

"This is amazing," he sighed as his body twisted and turned to each side.

Jimmy skulked around the corner, William's blissful roll was interrupted and he scrambled to his feet.

"We were just going to the gate," William said with a smidgeon of panic. Jimmy cast an imposing shadow and his look was enough to send them straight to the gate.

Chapter Two

William and Sam had been sitting by the gate for a while now but nobody else had come and left the gate open. They were starting to get bored.

"Shall we go and see where Lewis and Millie are?" William asked.

"Hmm," Sam was not sure, she did not want any repeats of the chicken disaster.

"I promise that I will stick to the rules, I won't scare any animals and I won't get into any more trouble," William reassured her. Sam was torn; she was really bored.

"Pleeeease," William pleaded.

Sam gave in and stood up, giving herself a shake.

"No trouble," she ordered.

"Absolutely not." William's eyes gleamed, he was confident that everything was going to be just fine.

They went for a wander and found Lewis and Millie mucking out stables in a big, airy barn. There were bales of straw stacked at the side of the barn. Sam jumped up.

"This is comfy," said Sam as she lay on the straw. It felt so soft and cosy, so she curled up, tucking her nose into her belly. The horses were out in the field for the moment, but they were able to walk freely in and out of their stables. They often took shelter from weather at night-time, so their stables needed checking for muck in the morning. William was mooching around with his nose skimming the ground as he continuously sniffed, picking up lots of different scents. Dogs have a fantastic sense of smell, a lot better than humans. They can easily get distracted by lots of different odours, especially when they are somewhere new. Suddenly, out of the corner of his eye, a quick movement caught his attention. He froze, standing still with his paw in the air, ready for action.

"What was that?" William was puzzled. He moved slowly, step by step over to the corner, stretching his nose out in front of him, sniffing the air to pick up the strange scent. There was a small gap in the wall, his eyes locked onto it. The stables were built from traditional stone which houses lots of holes, nooks and crannies; anything could be behind them. William was fascinated, he could not see into the gap so pawed at the wall. He stopped and used his nose again to find out if he could smell anything around the gap. Something the other side of the gap touched his nose, William jumped and leapt backwards. But curiosity made him go back to the gap. Dogs, after all, are inquisitive creatures. He crept over to see what it was that had touched his nose. It was another nose but it was much smaller than his, in fact it was tiny.

"Hello," William said hesitantly.

"What do you want?" a small voice squeaked back cautiously. It was a field mouse. Mice can be common around farms as there are lots of grass and woodlands for them to get plenty of nuts, seeds and berries. But they are very timid, so spotting one can be difficult, especially as they are normally nocturnal.

"I just wondered what you were. Do you live here?" William asked.

"Why?" replied the mouse, who still was not sure why William had followed him home, he didn't want his stash of seeds being stolen. Mice are very wary; they are prey animals and cats do like to hunt them. The mouse certainly did not want to end up being dinner.

"I only wanted to say hello, I don't want to harm you," William assured the mouse. This was true, William liked to meet new animals and would not normally harm anything. The mouse however was suspicious, quite rightly as many dogs would instinctively have hunted the mouse. The mouse suddenly leapt backwards using its huge back feet, perfect for jumping, and quick as a flash went back inside its home.

"Don't go," William pleaded, but the mouse was gone. William sniffed the gap again. All of a sudden, he felt tense; sensing a presence behind him he went rigid and turned apprehensively. A cat. He now understood why the mouse had disappeared so suddenly. Dogs are not the only working animals on farms, some also have cats to catch rodents. The cat was making herself look as tall as possible, her sleek black fur was standing on end, her tail was stiff and curled round creating the letter c, c for crazy. Her ears were flat against her head. She was staring at William through her narrowed green eyes, they pierced through William, a sure sign that she was annoyed.

"What are you doing?" The cat hissed, annoyed that this stranger was apparently trying to steal her job from her.

"I was just saying hello to the mouse." William's ears and head sank and he inched backwards away from the cat. She did not look like she should be approached.

"Finding mice is my job." She hissed again, her long elegant legs stretching out in front of her as she walked slowly and boldly towards William. William's heart was beating faster now, he wasn't sure who to be more afraid of, this cat or Jimmy.

*"For I am Camila, Camila the killer cat,
Do you know what I do if I see a rat?
I gobble it up, it is so tasty and nice,
I do exactly the same if I see any mice."*

William carried on walking backwards, he now understood why the mouse would not say hello with a predator like Camila on the prowl.

"I'm sorry, I didn't actually want it for dinner."

Camila was still approaching William, she hissed again baring her teeth.

Thankfully, the clip-clopping of horse's shoes came around the corner of the barn and broke the tension.

"I hope you are playing nicely Camila," Molly said as she was leading the horse back to the stable. Camila gave a final hiss at William and ran over to Molly, brushing herself against Molly's legs. Her whole posture had changed to one of a much happier cat. Her ears were now up and her body was now relaxed, her muscles were no longer tense.

"Thank you, Molly, just in time. Another nanosecond and I would have been cat food. Boy those claws looked sharp." William felt a massive sense of relief.

Molly had brought one of the horses in, Tommy, because she had promised the children a ride in return for their hard work. Lewis was looking forward to his birthday ride today. Sam was not taking any chances and stayed high up on the straw, she did not want those big metal shoes anywhere near her.

"Wow, he's massive." William joined Sam on the straw and was in awe at the size of the majestic animal walking in. Tommy may be big, but he was very gentle and would not intentionally stand on a dog, or person for that matter. The lead rope Molly was using to lead him was quite long. Tommy had spotted the little white dogs on the straw and wandered over; he nickered, his ears pointing forward. He stretched his neck forward and put his head down so that his nose was very close to William's nose. It was the second time today William had been nose to nose with another animal, except this nose was much bigger than the nose of the mouse and, in fact, is called a muzzle. Horses have lots of whiskers on their muzzles; these are very sensitive and allow them to feel things in their surrounding environment. So, unlike men who shave, they should never be shaved off. Tommy wiggled his muzzle on William; horses like to do this when they are investigating things. William quite liked this sensation; it was like having a post to scratch on without having to do the work for himself. Tommy's breath smelt sweet from the pasture that he had been grazing on.

"Hello," William greeted Tommy, slightly wary of his size. William then sniffed to carry on his greeting, but his fur must have tickled Tommy because Tommy sneezed all over him.

"Urgh, that was gross," he said and went to wipe his head in the straw. That was the second time today that his head had been covered with something yucky. If he was not careful, he could be getting a bath when they got home and he certainly did not want that. He decided he would be very careful to keep clean from now on.

"Sorry about that," Tommy apologised. He then took a sneaky mouthful of straw. The straw was used as bedding and was not meant to be food, but horses love a mixture of things to graze on.

"Do you ever stop eating?" William asked. Tommy explained,

"In the paddock grazing is how we like to spend our time.
If we can graze for 16 hours a day then this is sublime.
Walking and roaming are very important to us,
If we are not allowed out then we will make a fuss."

"Gosh, that's a long time to eat." William was surprised, "I would love to spend 16 hours a day eating biscuits."

"You would get far too fat." Sam put a dampener on his fantasy.

Lewis, excited to ride, walked behind Tommy and scratched his hindquarters. This made Tommy jump a little.

"Now just a note of caution about our eyesight,
Approach us from the side so we don't get a fright.
Our eyes are big, but directly behind us we cannot see.
If you scare us, we may kick out and in pain you will flee."

Sam absorbed this information; she definitely did not want to get kicked.

Molly then led Tommy away to tie him up so the children could brush him and tack him up.

Molly was helping Millie to put the bridle on Tommy. Tommy was very helpful and put his head down to allow Millie to put the bridle on but Millie could not reach high enough to put the saddle on, so Lewis stepped in. Millie had borrowed a riding hat from Molly. She put this on and secured the chin strap so that the hat sat safely on her head. Millie then put gloves on to stop the reins slipping through her fingers when she was riding and led Tommy to the mounting block. The mounting block had three wooden steps leading up to a platform where Millie could climb up and stand, making it much easier for her to mount Tommy. Once she was on, she gently nudged Tommy with her heels to encourage him to walk forward. They walked into the paddock where Molly would be giving them a lesson. Sam and William walked to the front of the barn. Tommy was far enough away now, so Sam was happy that she would not get stood on.

Outside the barn was another horse, the lead rope was tied to some string attached to the wall of the barn.

"Crikey, that horse's foot is burning!" Sam was shocked, her eyes wide with concern. There was smoke billowing from the horse's hoof. A man was bent over beside the horse clasping his foot between his thighs. To the uneducated eye it could look like the man was hurting the horse as smoke is associated with fire. William dashed over.

"Are you okay? Can we help you? Shall I get Fred?" William spilled the questions out as fast as he could; he urgently wanted to protect the horse from this abominable act of cruelty.

"Oh, I'm fine!" replied the horse. "He's not hurting me, he's a farrier," the horse continued to explain.

"What's a farrier?" William was captivated, he desperately wanted to know why it was okay that smoke was coming from the horse's foot.

"A farrier is the person who is in charge of keeping our hooves in top-notch shape," the horse explained.

> "Our hooves are like your nails, they constantly grow,
> So, trimming and balancing they must undergo.
> This makes sure they don't get overgrown and sore,
> Otherwise, we will be lame and this we abhor."

The farrier carried on trimming the horse's hooves with a rasp. He heated the shoes in his forge and then shaped them on the anvil, making sure each shoe was the perfect fit. Once they were, the farrier nailed the shoe to the hoof.

"So that's how they fit a metal shoe to a horse." Sam was fascinated by the process.

Now they knew that the horse was fine they went to the edge of the paddock and watched Millie and Tommy going around in circles. Camila was walking along the fence, her tail keeping her perfectly balanced, she walked past and glared at William.

"Let's go," William said. He was truly hoping that Camila would not tell Jimmy what had happened, he did not want his dreams of becoming a farm dog to be over, not just yet. But William was too eager to leave and, as he jumped up to run off, the sudden movement and noise gave Tommy a fright. Horses are fight or flight animals; Tommy chose flight and launched himself into the air, cantering hastily to the other side of the paddock. This knocked Millie off balance. She was not ready for the sudden increase in speed and took a sharp intake of breath before squealing with terror, her heart thumping.

"Hold on tight Millie!" Molly called out, hoping this would save her from falling. Millie held on to the front of the saddle for dear life, gripping as tightly as she could to stop herself plummeting to the ground; she definitely did not want to make such an unglamorous dismount. Tommy came to a halt at the fence. Both Millie and Molly sighed with relief.

"Well done, Millie, you gripped like a vice there!" Fred was walking past grinning and gave Millie a wink of approval. "What's up with you Tommy?" He grabbed Tommy's reins over the fence so that Millie could steady herself. Tommy snorted and shook his head.

William scurried off stealthily to avoid frightening Tommy again, he had done little to impress anybody so far.

Chapter Three

Safely out of sight, William wanted to find something fun to do.

"What shall we do now Sam?"

"I don't know," she replied. "We could go into the fields for a bit." She thought this might keep William out of trouble, so off they scampered towards the fields. They had walked past a bucket of water on the way which was meant for the horses. It was taller than they were so they had to stand on their back legs with their front paws on the rim of the bucket to lap up some water.

There was a hedgerow in between the fields. Fred and Molly liked to make sure that there were lots of places for the wildlife to live around the farm as well as looking after their own farm animals, so they had planted lots of hedges to encourage the wildlife to find a home. William and Sam were sniffing around the bottom of the hedge excitedly searching for a place to squeeze through. William pressed deeper into the hedge.

"Hey, watch out!" A voice hissed and the animal swiftly curled into a tight ball, the crisp leaves rustled with the sudden movement. William jumped backwards; he had bumped into a hedgehog and had hurt himself in the process.

"Ouch!" cried William. The hedgehog was covered in lots of prickly spines and had promptly curled into a ball when William got too close. This was a way of protecting itself; if William had been a badger, the hedgehog would have been dinner.

"I didn't mean to scare you," William was panicking. He didn't want Jimmy to find out that he had scared yet another animal.

"I was sleeping," the hedgehog was rather miffed. Hedgehogs are nocturnal animals so they normally sleep through the day and search for food at night. He was having a lovely sleep under the hedge, the twigs and fallen leaves make a great bed for hedgehogs so it was a perfect place to rest. The hedges were also full of lots of insects, snails and slugs for them to feast on.

"We wanted to get to the next field," William wanted to explain why he had disturbed him, "Please come out." William tried to persuade the hedgehog to unravel himself. The hedgehog, sure that he was now safe, uncurled. His black nose on the end of his pointed snout was so shiny it looked like it had been polished. His small round eyes looked apprehensively at William.

"That's amazing, how do you do that?" William was mightily impressed with that talent.

> "We have two large muscles either side of our back,
> So we can curl up tightly in case of attack.
> This makes our quills stand on end,
> And from frightful predators we can defend."

William wished he could do that, especially at bath time. Sam, who had taken great interest in how the hedgehog had defended itself, was standing next to the hedge. A butterfly then landed on her nose, startling her a little. Butterflies are supposed to be active during the day so at least the dogs hadn't disturbed this animal. Sam's eyes almost crossed as she tried to focus on her, she was taken with her beauty. The butterfly continued to flap her wings slowly; she had exquisite zesty orange wings with black dots and shapes, the tips were black with white dots. Even though dogs can't see as many colours as humans, Sam still knew she was pretty.

"You're beautiful," Sam told the butterfly.

"Thank you, I'm a painted lady," replied the butterfly, full of pride. She flapped her wings again to show off her colours and flew into the air. Sam stood up on her hind legs in an attempt to follow the butterfly but she could not tell which one had landed on her. The butterflies were abundant as the sun was out today. It needs to be a certain temperature for the butterflies to be able to fly, so the sun had brought them all out. The hedgehog, now awake, took lots of interest in the butterfly, he does like to eat insects but would normally eat the caterpillar before it had metamorphosed into a butterfly. But the butterfly was too quick and flew away before the hedgehog could try anything. The hedgerow was definitely a haven for wildlife. Apologising to the hedgehog again for waking him, the dogs crawled through the hedge and went into the next field.

They walked through the field in which the horses were kept, being sure to avoid their blind spot, and scuttled underneath the lowest rail of the post and rail fence. They noticed some funny-shaped buildings in the next field.

"I wonder what they're for." Sam did not know what it was

they were looking at. The buildings were made of metal and were shaped like an arch.

"Maybe something lives in them," suggested William. They surveyed the field and spotted some rather large animals. The animals were pink with brown patches on them and had funny curly tails; neither William nor Sam had seen any animals like them before.

"Gosh, what are they?" asked Sam.

"I don't know, let's go and talk to them," suggested William. He had recovered from his meeting with Camila, and besides, these animals looked much more chilled. Sam was not sure and wondered whether they could be dangerous.

But as William likes to talk to everything he meets, he ignored Sam and scooted off in the direction of the animals. Sam sighed wearily and reluctantly followed him. Before they could reach the animals, William and Sam heard voices. Fred had walked down to the field with Lewis and they were both carrying buckets. Lewis had said that Millie could have the first ride as he wanted to help Fred feed the pigs. William and Sam sauntered over to them to find out what they were doing there. William was interested in what was in the buckets. As Lewis was shorter than Fred, his buckets were closer to the ground so William decided to inspect those.

"Hey, that food is not for you, William, it's for the pigs," Fred laughed as William stuck his nose in.

"Oh, they're pigs," William told Sam.

The pigs had heard Fred walking over with buckets and knew this meant food. Their vision is not always great, but they have good hearing and sense of smell. They trotted over, grunting happily. Fred told Lewis to scatter the food on the floor. The food was a mix of vegetables and their specially made pig pellets. William went to investigate the food on the floor.

"Oi, that's our food," one of the pigs shouted at William. William quickly apologised and backed away, he did not want to make the pig angry like Camila had been, even if the pigs' food was much more appealing.

William and Sam sat back and watched the pigs scoff the food; they were using their strong snouts to root through the food and were making satisfying grunting noises. Although William liked some vegetables, especially carrots, he was not going to try and take any.

Once the pigs had finished eating, which did not take long, William tried to talk to them.

"Hello, my name's William, I'm a Westie," he introduced himself to the pig that had told him off for trying to eat the food. He thought it best to try and make friends; he did not know how friendly this pig was with Jimmy. "What is your name?"

"My name is Pierre, Pierre the Portly Pig," he replied proudly. Pigs often carry extra body fat as this helps them to keep warm in cold weather, hence he was portly. They sniffed each other, Pierre's blue, eager eyes were searching William. William was looking into Pierre's snout, his round nostrils almost looked like another pair of eyes as Pierre wriggled his snout from side to side, they were much smaller than Tommy's nostrils.

"What do you do?" William asked. He explained to William.

> *"We use our snout to forage and root for food,*
> *This always puts us in a good mood.*
> *We wallow in the mud, but this does not mean we're dirty,*
> *It keeps us cool and happy, which makes our tails curly."*

Pierre was much friendlier now that William was not trying to eat his food.

"Come on, I'll show you my house."

They went to Pierre's house. After tipping the food out of the buckets, Fred and Lewis had walked back across the field to carry on with other chores and so did not notice William and Sam mooching off with the pig. Pierre led them into his home, known as a pig ark.

"Gosh, this is much bigger than our bed." William looked around the spacious home. There was no grass inside, just lots of straw so that the pigs could keep warm and root around.

"We also have a muddy wallow in the field," Pierre said boastfully and led them to it.

"You're allowed to roll around in here and you don't get told off?" William asked, astonished.

"Of course we don't get told off, that's what we do," Pierre replied. William thought this was marvellous and could not believe how lucky the pigs were; he was overcome with envy.

"Sometimes the farmers spray us with hose pipes as well," Pierre exclaimed joyfully. William did not think this was quite as lucky though as he was not keen on being sprayed with water, having a bath or anything which involved cleaning him.

"Hey, you've got toys." William noticed a rubber ball in the field.

"Pigs like to play, too, you know," Pierre replied. With that William dropped his front legs to the floor, leaving his haunches high and wagging his tail, the pose a dog strikes when they are eager to play, called a play bow. He then ran over to the ball. He gave it a good sniff before picking it up in his mouth and running over to Sam. Sam chased William trying to get the ball from him. William was darting this way and that, trying to avoid Sam and keep her from stealing the ball.

"You can't catch me," William gloated between gritted teeth.

"Don't run away with my ball," yelled Pierre. He was also eager to play but it was impossible for him to match the play bow, so he picked up the nearest toy to him. Fred and Molly put lots of different toys in the field for the pigs which they rotated so that the pigs did not get bored with them. This enriched their environment and allowed them to explore and have fun. Pierre started chewing a toy made of tough rubber and tied into a big knot. William noticed this and decided that the new toy looked like more fun so he ran over to Pierre.

"Let me have a go," he said to Pierre. But Pierre was not letting this toy go; he stuck his nose high into the air. William jumped up to try and get the toy out of Pierre's mouth. This amused Pierre and he stuck his snout even higher in the air. Pigs are very intelligent animals and he knew how to outwit this dog.

"You can't reach," he snorted and kept turning his head to either side. Both animals were having fun and playing; different species can play together. However, to an onlooker it could look like William was tormenting the pig. This is exactly what it looked like to Jimmy. Jimmy may live on the farm but he did not play with the animals; it was his job to keep things in order. He sprinted with the speed of a gazelle.

"Uh oh, incoming," Pierre said, dropping the toy.

"What do you mean?" William was puzzled.

"Jimmy's on his way and he doesn't look too happy," Pierre mumbled. William span round, he didn't know quite what he had done but he knew by the way Jimmy was hurtling towards him that he was in trouble again.

"Oh no, he hates me." William's disappointment grew. "I've already been told off for scaring a chicken, I didn't mean to though." William explained to Pierre.

"Don't be too hard on him," Pierre said, "Jimmy is very protective of them and of all the animals now. A few years ago, a fox got into the chicken coop and killed the chickens, Jimmy has never forgiven himself."

"But that's not his fault, is it?" questioned William.

"No, Fred and Molly had brought somebody in to look after all of us while they were away for a couple of days. Unfortunately, one night they didn't lock the door to the coop properly. But Jimmy took it really hard, he doesn't think it should have happened with him around and now he is ultra-protective of all the animals." Pierre's sad tale certainly explained why Jimmy was so adamant about defending the animals.

"William, what are you doing, you do not tease the animals," Jimmy scolded. William jumped back at hearing Jimmy so angry.

"I wasn't teasing him, we were only playing," William protested. "He had a nice toy."

"The toys belong to the pigs, they are not for you to play with. Now come away from him and leave them alone," Jimmy ordered. William, once again on the wrong side of Jimmy, hung his head, tucked his tail between his legs and walked back underneath the post and rail fence.

"Bye Pierre, it was nice to meet you."

"Bye William, hope to see you again," replied Pierre. Jimmy was surprised at this response. Maybe William had not been teasing him after all, but Jimmy still didn't like William. William's disappointment grew. Jimmy had such a bad impression of William; he thought his dream of becoming a farm dog was all but over.

Chapter Four

As William left the field feeling rather solemn, he heard a strange noise coming from the bottom of the field.

"Jimmy, here boy," Fred called across the field. Jimmy hesitated, he was torn as he did not want to leave William and Sam but he couldn't disobey Fred.

"Come on, we need to go back up," Jimmy told them.

"He didn't call us, only you," William said smugly. He didn't want Jimmy following them around. Jimmy glared at him, his muzzle twitching. William looked away wishing he hadn't been quite so cocky. Jimmy ran up the field towards Fred, shooting a warning glance at William as he left.

"What did you say that for?" Sam asked sounding a bit aggravated. She didn't want to ruffle any feathers and knew Jimmy should not be antagonised.

"Well, he's gone now," William dismissed her question. "Come on, let's go." He headed towards the direction of the noise.

As they got closer, they noticed that there was a river running across the bottom of Fred and Molly's land. The noise was the ducks quacking on the river, they were dipping their heads under water and wiggling their back ends which made William and Sam laugh. As they were watching the ducks, a frog leaped up the bank and William and Sam both jumped back in surprise. The frog croaked, William tilted his head and cautiously walked forward. The frog had dappled skin and long, powerful back legs; it had many predators so needed strong legs to hop away quickly. It could not trust William. William stretched his neck forward and sniffed the frog to investigate more, he licked its back, it did not taste good. The animal hopped forward again so William hopped backwards, the frog was not sure who was being more cautious.

"Are you going for a swim?" the frog asked. He had seen Jimmy diving into the river before and thought that's why these new dogs were here.

"Absolutely not!" Clearly the frog had no idea how displeasing that idea was to William. The frog had been feasting on insects and its long tongue came shooting out of its mouth.

"Gosh, that was quick." William was fascinated.

The frog explained,

"We have long sticky tongues to capture our dinner,

Slugs, snails and worms are always a winner.

To help keep us safe, our skin can change colour,

Depending on our surroundings it can be lighter or duller."

William found the frog's tongue very interesting. "Is that what the ducks are doing in the river?" he asked the frog.

"No, they feed a different way," he explained,

"Ducks have lamellae on the edge of their bill,
These get rid of water but keep food for their meal.
They eat seeds, berries, plants, anything that they see,
They will even eat small creatures, including frogs like me!"

"Oh, you'd best be careful then." William felt some concern for the frog, but the frog leapt away into the apparent safety of the reeds. William continued to sniff around and came across a nest. There were some very young ducklings in there. William was so excited to see them he sniffed around them and pawed at them. This wreaked havoc in the nest. The ducklings were terrified and started running and dispersing around the river bank. The mother duck was in the river feeding and flew over quacking fiercely at William.

"Get away from my babies," she yelled at him and tried to round up her ducklings. A fisherman on the bank on the other side of the river saw the commotion and yelled at William,

"Oi, leave the ducklings alone," he shouted. There was not much he could do from the other side of the bank but he was hoping his shouting would put William off chasing them. William didn't know which one to play with first as they tore around the bank. They were so cute with their furry yellow faces and brown furry bodies, they looked just like a cuddly toy. Except they were live animals being terrified by William's actions.

"Jump into the river," the mother duck instructed her panicking babies. One by one they went to the edge of the river, braced themselves and jumped into the river, trying to get to safety. The fisherman was encouraging the ducklings. Jimmy heard a stranger's voice shouting and pelted back down the field. He saw the disruption that William had caused to the ducklings,

"I didn't do anything, I just saw them in their nest," William flustered.

"They shouldn't be disturbed," Jimmy said with contempt. "Leave now, we can't have strangers thinking there are badly behaved dogs on this farm." Jimmy didn't want William's behaviour to be associated with the farm and was concerned the fisherman would think that William lived there.

"There you are, all safe now," the fisherman was offering comforting words to the ducklings. They were still swimming in circles staying close to their mother.

"Just leave them all alone." Jimmy's frustration was mounting, he didn't know how much more he could take of William. William lowered his ears; he felt sorry for himself again. From now on he would try really hard to impress Jimmy.

Chapter Five

"Don't be sad William," Sam tried to cheer him up. "Jimmy was only looking after the animals, but at least Pierre enjoyed himself."

"He did, didn't he?" William cheered up again thinking about the fun he and Pierre had had. Jimmy was still with them, prowling around. He didn't want to leave them on their own again after witnessing William's unwanted behaviour for a third time. They were walking along the fence line when Sam spotted some more animals. The animals were very big, bigger than the pigs and were black and white.

"What are they Jimmy?" asked Sam.

"They're called cows," Jimmy replied. "That's where milk comes from," he continued. "You can make cheese, butter and yoghurt from the milk too." William and Sam were learning a lot today. They were mainly fed dog food but sometimes, as a treat, they were allowed a piece of cheese which they loved.

"Can we go and say hello?" William asked.

"No!" snapped Jimmy. "Haven't you learnt anything? Besides, cows don't have very good eyesight and you don't want to get trampled by one of them." Jimmy only went into the field when he was with Fred.

"Lunchtime," Molly was heard calling from the farmhouse door.

"Yummy, come on guys," and with that Jimmy sprinted back up to the house for lunch.

"Come on William, let's go." Sam was eager to go back to the farmhouse for two reasons. Firstly, she was hungry after the morning's adventures and was quite excited about lunch. Secondly, she did not want William to get told off again by the scary Jimmy.

She wanted to get William back up to the house with everybody else.

"Can't we just go and say hello to a cow first?" William asked tentatively. He was desperate to go and meet one of these big animals, especially now he knew they made one of his favourite treats, cheese.

"No, you heard what Jimmy said. We don't want one of them to stand on us." Sam spoke firmly, she was being very cautious as she had been with the horses.

"I'll be careful," William promised. Then disregarding Sam, he slipped under the bottom rail, trotting off some distance to approach a cow. A cow spotted William, mooed, leaped in the air whilst shaking its head and charged at William. William span round as quick as a spinning top and ran as fast as he could back to the fence.

"Run William, hurry up!" cried Sam, urging William to reach the fence before the cow caught up with him. The cow was cantering at some speed. On noticing this, other cows began to join in and soon, most of the herd was chasing William. Sam could barely watch; she was desperate for William to reach the fence. It sounded like it was thundering as the cows' hooves pounded the ground. William got underneath the rail before the cows could reach him. They screeched to a halt just before the fence. They peered over the fence to get a closer look at William, their necks were stretched down with ears facing forward. William jumped back at the huge noses coming towards him, he could see right up their nostrils. Large white strips down the centre of their faces were covered in silky white hair.

"I'm sorry, I didn't mean to scare you, I just wanted to say hello," the cow that started the stampede said. She had beautiful long eyelashes, which opened up her huge, spirited eyes. The cows were not being nasty; cows have an inquisitive nature and they were just curious.

"What's your name?" asked William, keen to make friends.

"Catherine, Catherine the curious cow," she replied, stretching her neck down to get a better look. She gave William a big lick and a wag of the tail. Much like dogs, cows wag their tails when they are happy. Catherine was still chewing a mouthful of grass.

"You chew your food for a long time." William was intrigued, dogs are not renowned for taking their time to eat their food and often wolf it down.

"We can bring food back up from our stomach to chew it more," Catherine replied.

"Urgh, that's gross!" William thought this sounded pretty disgusting, but it helps the animals digest their food.

"It's called ruminating. Goats and sheep do it too." Catherine wanted William to know that it was normal for some animals. She went on to explain.

> *"Feeding, ruminating and lying down is how we like to spend our time,*
> *Spending half the day grazing and the other half resting is absolutely divine.*
> *Our digestive system is special, we are known as a ruminant,*
> *This means we regurgitate, re-chew and re-swallow, which other animals can't.*
> *We also produce lots of milk, which means we are milked every day, twice.*
> *For this we go to the milking parlour where they use a special device."*

"Oh wow, that's really interesting and I love cheese." William wanted Catherine to know that he appreciated her hard work. Some of the cows hadn't joined in and remained lying down in the shade of the trees. As Catherine said, they are often seen lying down and not because it is likely to rain, but this is an important time for them to ruminate and rest their feet.

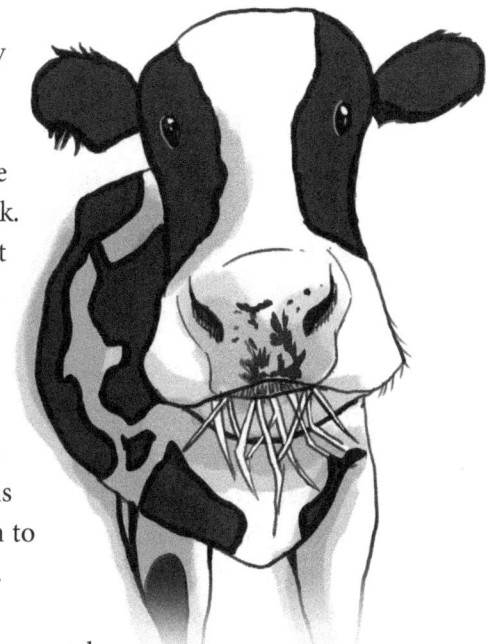

"Do you have to wear metal shoes too?" Sam asked Catherine. She was remembering the horse's explanation.

"No no," Catherine laughed. "Cows don't wear shoes, nobody rides us. Our hooves are different anyway, look," she instructed Sam.

"Oh, you have two bits!" Sam was surprised. The cow's hoof looked much different to the horse's hoof.

"Yes, we have cloven hooves, unlike the horses our hooves are split into two and each side is called a claw." Sam stepped back on hearing the word claw. Catherine laughed.

"Don't worry, they're not sharp, we won't hurt you," Catherine reassured her.

"Not like Camila's," thought William.

One of the cows clearly had an itch as she started rubbing

furiously on the fence post.

"Oh, that feels so good," she announced. Cows love to rub their head and bodies on the fence posts. William and Sam laughed, cows must love scratching as much as dogs, except William and Sam had Lewis and Millie to scratch them on command. They were so amused by watching the cow and how much pleasure she was getting out of it they didn't notice Jimmy reappear at the top of the field.

He was wondering what was taking the other dogs so long to come up for lunch. He could not understand as he was never late for lunch. Luckily, William was no longer in the cow field and they had just turned around to start to wander up to the farmhouse.

"Come on, what's taken you so long?" asked Jimmy.

"Nothing," replied Sam. "We were just having a mooch round." She didn't want William being told off again. Jimmy had specifically told him not to go into the cow field and he could easily have been trampled. Jimmy did not really believe that they had not been up to anything, he scanned the land with his beady eyes. The cows were all congregating at the fence but everything seemed in order so he went back into the farmhouse with William and Sam. Mum, Dad and the children were sitting down at the dining table ready for lunch. Molly and Fred had prepared a large feast to satisfy the appetites of everybody as they had been working hard all morning. There were different types of homemade bread with large chunks of cheese, hardboiled eggs, a plate of various meats and bowls of salad and fruit. It was a spread fit for royalty.

"This looks delicious," exclaimed Dad, his eyes lit with glee. Dad, like most dads, was always thinking about his stomach and piled his plate high with a variety of the delicious foods. He was the first to tuck in.

"Do we get any of that?" Sam asked William. But before he could reply, Molly came over.

"Hello you two, I've put some lunch in a bowl for you." She showed them where their lunch was.

"Wow, look at this." Sam was very excited at the bowl of food which was on the floor for them. They had their own lunchtime feast; not only were there dog biscuits, but there was some meat and vegetables. This was especially exciting as William and Sam did not normally eat at lunchtime; they had breakfast, and dinner in the evening. The dogs put their heads in their bowls and scoffed the food as if they hadn't eaten in a month. Their heads did not come up until the bowls had been licked so clean that they could see their reflections in them.

"That was yummy," declared Sam, and William enthusiastically agreed. The humans were still at the table eating, so William and Sam joined Jimmy on the large mat in the living room, much to his annoyance. He wasn't used to sharing his rug with other dogs and didn't see why he had to today. They wiped their mouths on it to get rid of the grease and then curled up for a post-lunch nap.

Conversation at the dinner table was about the morning's activities, the children were talking very enthusiastically and passionately.

"What was your favourite part of the morning?" Molly asked the children.

"Riding the horse," Millie replied even though she had had a bit of a fright. Molly laughed, she knew that would be the answer.

"What about the jobs you have been doing?" asked Fred.

"I liked feeding the pigs," answered Lewis.

"Collecting the eggs," Millie responded. "Are these the eggs that we collected?" Millie asked Molly as she bit into a hardboiled egg.

"Yes, they are, completely fresh from the hen house," Molly told her. Millie felt happy that she had contributed to lunch in a small way.

"What are we going to do after lunch?" asked Lewis, curious to find out his afternoon tasks. He was definitely enjoying his birthday outing.

"We need to go and check the sheep," Fred told him. "There are some lambs as well, so we need to make sure that they are okay."

"Can I come and see the lambs?" asked Millie. She loved animals, in particular she loved baby animals and was filled with enthusiasm about seeing some little lambs.

"Of course you can," Fred told her, laughing at her eagerness. Needless to say, he liked animals, but he saw them every day. It was nice to have people so excited on the farm. Mum was also thrilled about seeing the lambs; she too loved baby animals and was hoping to meet one of them in the afternoon. William and Sam pricked up their ears, baby animals sounded like fun.

Chapter Six

Once everybody had finished lunch, they cleared the table and got ready to do an afternoon of work. The noise of the clearing up alerted the dogs that lunchtime was over. They slowly rose to their feet and all had a big stretch.

"I feel better after that nap," declared William as he gave a vigorous shake. He was ready to go exploring again now.

"Me too," Sam replied and the two walked into the kitchen to be greeted with cuddles from Lewis and Millie. The children along with Mum and Dad put their wellington boots back on and followed Fred. As Mum was walking out of the door, something caught her eye. As she turned her head, her eyes met the eyes of a large black spider, all eight of them. Mum drew in her breath and let out the most chilling scream. Mum was definitely not a fan of spiders. Fred jumped, grabbing his heart; he was not used to such an alarming reaction to a small animal. Dad laughed. He knew exactly what that scream was about; he had heard it hundreds of times.

"Crikey, what was that for?" Fred chuckled. Mum had already run to the other side of the kitchen; there was no way that she was walking past a spider that big.

"Get rid of it!" she shouted. Her voice still shaking with terror.

"You can't have a farm without spiders," Fred smiled. "It's not that big, look," he tried to sound reassuring, "pretty small really."

"Pretty small, pretty small!" Mum was not impressed. "Gargantuan more like." Mum was astounded that Fred had described this humungous beast as pretty small.

"Why do they even exist anyway?" Mum asked. She hated the scary creatures with a passion.

"Actually, spiders are very helpful and they are much smaller than you so you shouldn't be scared of them." Mum did not find this helpful.

"How are they useful?" Millie asked. She was not too keen on spiders either but was interested in the useful jobs that they carried out.

Fred explained,
> "They eat lots of insects that would eat the crops,
> But for them, there would be less food in the shops.
> Eating insects helps stop diseases spreading too,
> They might be more popular if only people knew!"

Fred was a big supporter of spiders, he picked it up and placed it outside.

"Off you go and find some food," he said as it scuttled away. Millie was impressed; she never knew spiders were so useful.

"I didn't know that, so they do lots of good work then."

"They certainly do. Come on, it's safe now," Fred smiled at Mum who still wasn't convinced and had stayed at a safe distance." Mum cautiously walked through the door.

"They may be good for the environment but that doesn't stop them from being creepy," she muttered.

"Are we going to see the lambs now?" asked Lewis.

"Yes, and I have a little surprise for you," replied Fred, a broad smile stretching across his cheeky face. Fred took them into a barn where there were some sheep and lambs in individual pens.

"Ahh, look at the little lambs!" Mum was taken with them.

"Now, this one isn't feeding too well at the moment," Fred explained as he picked up one of the lambs. "We've had to feed him milk in a bottle to make sure he's getting enough nutrition. Lewis, would you like to give him his bottle today?" Lewis was absolutely delighted that Fred trusted him to feed the lamb.

"Yes please," he shrieked. Fred lifted the lamb and showed Lewis how to hold the lamb properly to keep him safe and comfortable. All animals need to be handled correctly as this can be very stressful for them, and sheep scare easily. Fred placed the bottle of milk in his hand. Lewis was surprised at how strongly the lamb suckled. He had to hold on to the bottle tightly, but he was happy and gently stroked the lamb as it continued to feed from the bottle.

William and Sam had followed them into the barn. Sam had curled up on the straw again.

"This is so comfortable," she stated. "I wish Mum would put some of this in our bed."

William was more intrigued with what Lewis was doing.

"I wonder what Lewis is feeding the lamb?" William said to Sam. William's nosiness got the better of him again and he went over to the straw bale where Millie was sitting. He put his front paws up on the bale and stretched his head up trying to sniff the bottle. He knew it was milk, he recognised the scent. He stretched his head even higher licking the air trying to reach the bottle, he could almost taste it.

"William, it's for the lamb," laughed Lewis and gently pushed him down.

"Come on then you two, out of the barn." Fred ordered them to leave. Sam was not impressed; she was nice and cosy and not causing any trouble.

"That was your fault, you should have left the bottle alone," she snapped at William.

"There was milk in it," William said trying to justify his behaviour. "Hey look, there are more lambs in the field." William noticed that, behind the barn, there was a field full of lambs and their mothers. The lambs in the field were older than those in the barn so had been turned out into the field.

"They do look cute," Sam said as they moseyed over to the fence. The sun was shining and the lambs were full of the joys of spring, leaping around completely carefree.

"That looks like fun," William and Sam laughed; the high spirits of the lambs were rubbing off onto the dogs. The dogs could not get into the field as there was meshed wire attached to the post and rail fence to stop any lambs escaping and to keep them safe from predators.

"I wish there was a way we could go and play with them," William said. Sam did not argue with this as she normally would as she really wanted to go and see the lambs too. William was sniffing around the bottom of the fence when he noticed a small hole in the wire and pawed at the ground.

"Hey, I reckon we could squeeze through here." William was ecstatic that he may have found a way in. He sank down onto his belly and crawled along the floor commando style, just managing to get through the hole.

"Come on Sam!" he urged his sister to follow him. Sam, although excited about meeting the lambs, suddenly felt unsure about following William through the fence. "What are you waiting for?" enquired William.

"I'm not sure we should be doing this? What if Jimmy catches us?" Sam was worried they would get into trouble again.

"Jimmy's busy. We're only going to say hello." William tried to persuade Sam to come through the hole.

In a shocking display of rebellion, the normally extremely

well-behaved Sam crawled through the hole to join William in the field. They may have been slightly exuberant in the way they tried to greet the lambs and probably should not have run at them so fast. The lambs and their mothers scurried away in the opposite direction. William really should have learnt from the episode with the chicken that morning.

"We're friendly, we only want to play," William shouted after them.

"Please don't run away, we're not going to hurt you." Sam joined in, trying to persuade the lambs and their mothers that they were actually friendly. She also knew Jimmy would go mad if he saw them scaring the animals. But the lambs and their mothers were not to be convinced. The sheep flocked together to protect each other and soon, because sheep follow each other and run when frightened, the whole field was filled with panic. They were running away as fast as they could.

A ewe called out,

> *"Horrible dogs get away from us,*
> *As sheep we find it hard to trust.*
> *Chasing us will make us extremely stressed,*
> *So leave our field, it's for the best."*

"This isn't working William, we're just scaring them. Stop running," she called after him. William realised that Sam was right and just as he was stopping, Jimmy suddenly appeared. With the grace of an Olympic show jumper, he leaped over the five-bar gate and charged at William. William froze, his muscles tensed but fear would not let him move. His lips were tightly shut, he whined as Jimmy approached him at high speed. William thought Jimmy was going to bowl him over, but Jimmy was agile and stopped directly in front of William.

"What are you doing? I specifically told you that I'm the only dog who's allowed to round up the sheep. You don't even know what you are doing!" Jimmy was visibly angry; his hackles were up and he was baring his teeth. His eyes were ablaze with anger as they pierced though William.

"You've misunderstood, I wasn't trying to round them up, we only wanted to say hello to the lambs, they looked so cute and happy." William was panicking and started to shake, he avoided eye contact, but Jimmy wasn't interested in listening to William's excuses. Jimmy had seen what he had seen and that was that.

"How did you get in here?" he barked, spitting the words out through gritted teeth.

"There was a hole at the bottom of the fence so we crawled

through it," William answered timidly.

"Well, I suggest you crawl back out again," Jimmy snapped. So, William and Sam sank onto their bellies and crawled back under the fence. Jimmy jumped back over the gate.

"If only Fred could understand me, I'd get you two thrown out." Luckily, Fred was still in the barn and hadn't seen all the commotion, or he probably would have made William and Sam leave the farm. Mum and Dad would not have been happy about that.

"We promise we won't go into any more fields, don't we William?" Sam was trying to make peace with Jimmy. She knew he was only protecting the animals.

"We promise." William was terrified of Jimmy now; he was very scary when he was angry.

Jimmy looked around at the sheep and saw them still in turmoil. Something inside him snapped, he couldn't bear to see them like that after he had worked so carefully with them. The anger bubbled up inside him and rose to the surface like a volcano about to erupt.

"How dare you scare them like that, I want you off my farm now," Jimmy exploded. William shook uncontrollably, he didn't know what to do, apart from the obvious, run! He whipped round, spotted the open gate to the driveway and ran as fast as he could. But he was no match for Jimmy's speed, Jimmy was bigger and quicker and was snapping at William's heels. William could feel the tips of Jimmy's teeth on his hind legs. He tried to run faster but he couldn't, he was running faster than he ever had and still Jimmy was there, snapping at him, shouting at him.

"You've been nothing but trouble since you first placed your paws on this farm and I'm not having it anymore. This is my farm.

You need to go and never come back." Jimmy couldn't see reason anymore, he just saw the disruption that William had caused to his animals and he needed to be dealt with, immediately. William was wailing as he bolted, he flew out of the gate hoping that would bring him to safety. Jimmy raced out after him. He flicked his snout under William's stomach which launched him into the air, William tumbled to the ground and was flipped onto his back. William was now helpless as Jimmy pinned him down with his paw, snapping and snarling in his face, the saliva drooling down. William struggled under the weight of Jimmy and was flinging himself around. He managed to dislodge Jimmy and scramble to his feet. The noise that the writhing created disturbed the birds who shot out of the hedges. The sound of the beating wings panicked William further; he didn't know what the sound was in the confusion and he darted across the driveway to avoid anything else that was trying to kill him. Jimmy didn't flinch and hurtled up the driveway behind him chasing him to the lane.

"Jimmy, stop!" William heard a voice laced with panic. Molly sounded as terrified as William was, she yelled at Jimmy again, "Jimmy, stop, now!" Jimmy obeyed. As much as he wanted to chase William and make sure that he never came back, Molly was his mistress so he stopped running and turned around to make his way back to the farm.

"What an earth are you doing?" she questioned Jimmy, shocked to see him pursuing poor William in this way. But Jimmy wasn't able to make her understand.

"I must go and find William," she was terrified that William was going to get hurt. William had carried on running; blind panic had set in and he daren't stop to check if Jimmy was still behind him.

Jimmy was demonic and William had to get away. His heart was pounding and his paws were getting sore, he couldn't feel Jimmy's presence anymore. Was it safe to stop? He looked behind him, Jimmy was no longer chasing him but he knew it wasn't safe to turn around and go back to the farm, Jimmy was a monster. Panic turned to fear, what was he going to do now? He heard another noise, the whirring of an engine. He looked in front of him; a car was hurtling down the lane. He had to get out of the way so he leapt into the hedge, hoping that he wouldn't have a painful landing like earlier. Phew, no hedgehogs. The car whooshed passed him. He was safe from that particular danger. He was panting hard from the chase, he had to figure out what to do now. He suddenly felt very alone. Would Mum and Dad find him? He stretched his legs out in front of him and rested on his belly. Maybe they would find him if he just waited. He pricked up his ears, he could hear his name:

"William, William!" Although he did not know her very well, he recognised the voice as Molly's, but it sounded different. The tone was higher and there was an urgency to it. He peered through the branches of the hedge, he sighed as he saw that she was on her own. He emerged from the hedge and shook off the debris.

"Oh William, thank goodness you are okay." Molly was tremendously relieved to see him in one piece. Of course, she was happy that he was safe, but she was very thankful to find him as he was somebody else's dog. She didn't know how she would have explained his disappearance as it was Jimmy's fault he had run away, and she didn't know why Jimmy would have done that.

She bent down and picked off the remaining leaves from his fur and tugged at a branch that had become entangled around his back legs. "You had a bit of a fright, didn't you?" She said gently and scooped him up into her arms. She gave him a gentle squeeze and he knew he was safe now. Molly hadn't seen Jimmy react like that before and she was angry that he had frightened their guest in such a way.

"Come on William, let's get you back to the farm." Molly continued to carry William back up the lane to the farm; she didn't have a lead for him and she didn't want to risk losing him again.

As Molly approached the gate, Sam was sitting there. The conflict had distressed her and she was desperate to know that William was okay. She stood on her back legs and waved with her front legs trying to greet him.

"Somebody's pleased to see you," Molly laughed as she gently placed William down.

"Oh William, I thought you were a goner." Sam comforted William by licking his face, pleased he was okay.

"Me too," William returned the greeting, although he was nervous to be back at the farm as Jimmy had been very clear that he was not to come back.

"Come on William, come on Sam," Molly encouraged them to come into the kitchen with her. "Out." She ordered Jimmy to leave the kitchen where he had been sulking, so that William and Sam could stay there in peace. Jimmy went out begrudgingly, sneering as he left. He would do anything for Fred and Molly. He had been fiercely loyal to them ever since they brought him back from the dogs' home. They had chosen him and he was forever grateful that they had provided him with such a lovely home and William was going to ruin that for him. He felt another surge of anger inside.

Molly scratched William and Sam under the chin.

"There, all safe now." They both sat down to encourage Molly to carry on making a fuss of them. If she had known how much they had scared the sheep, she certainly wouldn't be making such a fuss of them or be angry at Jimmy.

Jimmy went to check that the ewes and the lambs were okay. They were starting to settle after their fright.

"What terrible dogs," one of the ewes commented.

"Don't worry," replied Jimmy, "I'll get them thrown out if it's the last thing I do, and I know just who to help me."

Chapter Seven

The dogs eagerly lapped up fresh, clean water from the bowl on the kitchen floor, they were thirsty after the stress of the chase. The water was so refreshing for them but their exuberance caused water to spill all over the floor. Whilst they were wondering what to do next and how to keep safe, Molly went to the front door and put her wellies on. She picked up a couple of buckets on her way out; one was empty and one was full of warm soapy water. She grabbed a towel and headed out of the door.

"William, Sam." She called them as she left the house. They rushed to join her, water dripping from their beards, keen to be by the safety of her side. She walked around the back of the house to a place where they had not yet been and walked towards an orchard. There were a few apple trees, however the branches were bare of the fruit as it was a bit too early in the year. Faced with a five-bar gate, Molly grasped the metal handle and pulled it out of its latch to open it. She allowed the dogs to go through the gate and closed it behind them.

Dad and Millie were in the paddock already, they were helping to build a new structure for the animals to play on under the guidance of Fred. They were all oblivious to the problem between Jimmy and William.

"This one is going to be fun," Dad said as they were preparing to tie planks of wood together. They were planning to build a suspension bridge held up by tying it to four stakes, two at either end. Fred had asked them to drill holes in the planks of wood so that rope would be able to feed through. Dad and Millie were busy fumbling with the tape measure to calculate where to drill the holes.

William and Sam came over and sniffed the planks of wood.

"Hello, you two," Dad ruffled their fur affectionately. "Still on your best behaviour I hope." William felt guilty as he accepted the affection. Dad would have been very disgruntled if he had known about the previous goings-on. William and Sam returned their attention to Molly.

"Look at those animals, what are they?" William asked Sam.

There were two brown and white animals in the corner of the orchard. They were on top of a big wooden structure, heads in the air, alert.

"I don't know but we probably shouldn't ask, let's just stay with Molly," Sam replied. She didn't want to upset Molly as well.

"Hello Gabriella, hello Gracie," Molly cheerfully greeted the animals as they came over and nuzzled her hand. She gave them a couple of treats as she stroked their sleek, shiny coats.

"Well, we know their names," Sam said. Molly placed the bucket with the warm soapy water underneath Gabriella and sat on a stool next to her that she kept in the orchard. She cleaned her udder with the warm soapy water. Once this was complete, she dried the udder then wrapped her fingers around the teat and gently squeezed. Milk shot into the empty metal bucket in rhythmical squirts, sounding almost musical as it hit the metal.

"That's not a different type of cow is it?" William questioned Sam. He recognised the white fluid as milk and had already learnt from Jimmy earlier that cows produce milk. William, who failed to get any milk from Lewis earlier, went and sat next to Molly.

"Hi, William, are you making friends with the goat?" Molly asked. The goats were quite used to dogs as Jimmy was always around somewhere.

"Oh, it's a goat." He thought that she looked very different from the cows in the field.

"It's a goat Sam," William called to Sam who had stayed further back. Gabriella turned her head round and looked at William, she did not normally have an audience whilst she was being milked.

"Hello," William greeted her, unsure how to greet a goat.

"Hello." The brusque reply signified that Gabriella was not impressed.

"We're just visiting the farm today. My name is William and that is my sister Sam sitting over there." Gabriella looked over to where Sam was sitting.

"Hello," Sam called nervously from a distance; she could sense the hostility towards them.

"Yes, we've heard about you two, you scared the sheep earlier," Gabriella said curtly through gritted teeth.

"We didn't mean to, honestly, we just wanted to play with the lambs and we accidently scared them," William spoke rapidly trying to vindicate himself.

"You have to be very careful around them, they are very timid," Gabriella told him. William looked down, he knew he had scared them and felt bad about his behaviour. However, they soon began chatting and Gabriella realised they were not so bad in spite of what she had heard. Gabriella was not shy like the sheep.

"What do you like to do?" William asked.

"We are Gabriella and Gracie the gregarious goats,
Having things to explore gets our vote.
We get easily bored so love our playground,
Over the obstacles we like to climb and bound."

"A playground!" William thought this sounded very exciting, "Can I see it please?"

"Absolutely." As soon as Molly had finished milking her, Gabriella hurried to the playground with William, excited to show it off. Goats like to be up high so it is important that they have things to climb on. William's eyes widened with elation, he was astonished at the playground before him. There were ramps with ridges on leading to different height platforms, a log pile, and some tyres which had been turned on their side and were half-buried in the ground. This was definitely going to be fun.

"Wow, this looks amazing." William sprinted up a ramp to reach the lowest platform. Gabriella went into play mode. She stood on her back legs and launched herself forward, leaping exuberantly. She dashed up the ramp to William. William turned and ran again, racing up the ramps to the highest platform.

"I'm the king of the castle, and you're the dirty rascal," he teased Gabriella as he stood tall on the highest platform. She wasn't far behind him and leaped up to join him. Gabriella put her head down and tucked her chin in moving forward towards William, she headbutted him.

"Hey, careful," William recoiled. Suddenly he was tense and panic set in a little. He wasn't used to such rough play and the fright from Jimmy was still on William's mind. He looked quickly around him and scooted back down the ramp, but he couldn't beat Gabriella to the bottom, she had leaped off the platform onto the ground and stood dauntingly before him. She had a commanding presence and William didn't want to aggravate her so he crouched down into a play bow and then ran in circles, skidding to a halt and turning to face Gabriella each time. Gabriella was leaping and running after him. In and out of the structures they chased each other until they were out of breath. William lay on his belly, panting, his tongue was hanging far out of his mouth. Headbutting can be a form of bullying by goats, but thankfully Gabriella had only been playing.

Gracie, who had been watching them playing whilst she was being milked came over and started nibbling on the hedge next to her.

"Don't you eat grass?" William asked.

"We do, but we like to eat lots of other things as well, hedges are good, and shrubs. We like hay too. Do you remember Gabriella when you ate the neighbour's garden?" Gracie giggled.

"I do, that was fun," Gabriella replied. She remembered fondly the day she had escaped from the paddock and proceeded to eat Mrs Wills' gorgeous garden.

"She was so upset, all her beautiful, colourful flowers gone." Gabriella did feel a bit bad about the flowers, but they were totally yummy so she didn't really regret it.

"Fred and Molly had to grovel for hours," laughed Gracie.

"And buy her a whole new garden," Gabriella sniggered. "They made sure the fences were properly secure after that so there was definitely no escaping. No more flowers for me." The goats did have lots of appropriate food to browse on though, so she couldn't feel too hard done by.

"What's going on over there?" Gracie was looking at Millie and Dad, who were getting wrapped up in rope. There was sweat trickling down Dad's back, he threw the rope to the ground and picked up a mallet instead.

"Millie, hold the stake in place please." He preferred hammering things anyway. He gave an almighty swing and hit the top of the stake with the mallet as hard as he could. The stake moved minimally into the ground and the sound reverberated around the paddock. He puffed and lifted the mallet again but the force of swinging the mallet back and the lack of grip sent the mallet sailing through the air and striking an apple tree. Fred took a sharp intake of breath and put his hands to his head. The squirrel currently residing in her drey in the tree scurried along a branch and leaped to safety into the next tree; it wasn't just William who inadvertently scared animals. There always seemed to be some collateral damage when Dad tried to do some DIY.

"Don't worry, everything's fine." Dad didn't know if he was trying to convince himself or everybody else. He sheepishly retrieved the mallet and completed pounding the stakes into the ground. He carefully knotted the final piece of rope around the stake and stood back to admire his work.

Gracie and Gabriella, who have to investigate everything, were thrilled to have a new addition to their playground. They eagerly sprang onto the bridge. Luckily it wasn't too high as the rope gave way and the goats ended up on the floor.

"Ah, guess that wasn't quite tight enough then?" puzzled Dad. Gabriella and Gracie bleated critically.

"William, Sam," Molly called. She was leaving the orchard so the dogs had to go.

"Thanks for the fun," William said to Gabriella.

"You're welcome," Gabriella responded. She was happy to have met the dogs despite what she had heard, although she wouldn't tell Jimmy this. She knew that he wouldn't compromise on how he felt about them so she thought it best to keep it a secret. She didn't know that Jimmy had been conjuring up a plan and had got the scariest of all the animals to help him.

Chapter Eight

William was feeling happier now. He had been content to follow Molly around for the last couple of hours and revel in the safety that she brought. Jimmy, however, was most annoyed as he had been unable to get to them. As William and Sam trotted around another corner of the farm, they noticed some more animals that they had not yet spoken to. They were amusing to watch, waddling around with little tails appearing to wag, just like theirs did, and their long elegant necks stretching high. They thought they looked very similar to the ducks that they had seen when they were by the river, but these were bigger and white. William, with his new-found assurance went over to speak to them. Sam went with him but was cautious; she didn't want to stray too far away from Molly as she still had a feeling of terror that Jimmy would ambush them.

"Excuse me, what are you?" asked William.

"We're geese," one of them responded. She seemed very friendly, even though geese can have a reputation for being scary. Some farms even use them to guard their property as they are very territorial.

"Why don't you live on the river?" William asked. Geese were waterfowl, just like ducks.

"We can live on land as we like to forage and graze on the grass around the farm. It's fine as long as we have access to water. Would you like to see our pond?" the goose asked.

"Yes please," replied William and was delighted to follow the goose as if he had no cares in the world. They arrived at a large pool of water.

"Is this where you go swimming?" Sam enquired.

"Yes, we love to have a swim and a dip."

There was a goose on the edge of the water, her neck was turned to the side and her beak was buried in her feathers.

"What is she doing?" Sam asked.

"To groom ourselves we preen our bodies using our beak,
This keeps our feathers waterproof, clean and looking sleek.
To do this we release oil from the base of our tail,
This also makes our feathers strong so in flight we cannot fail.
We align our feathers and put them in the best possible position,
This helps us to protect ourselves against all weather conditions."

"She is certainly doing a good job," Sam observed.

William went to the edge of the water and pawed at it. It was murky from the sediment at the bottom.

"Don't go in William, it's for the geese," Sam scolded. They'd had a pleasant afternoon with Molly and she did not want it getting spoilt by William upsetting the geese.

"I'm not going to," he retorted, "I'm not a Labrador am I!" He did not mind having a little paddle, and certainly did not mind getting muddy, but getting completely wet was another matter, and something he did not enjoy, unlike some other dogs. But the geese did not know that, and jumped into the water, raised their bodies flapping their wings from the side to the front, splashing William. William jumped back quickly. He had been taken by surprise with the soaking. He shook himself to get rid of the water.

"Sorry," called one of the geese. "Why don't you come in, it's not very deep," she tried to reassure him. William was a bit wary about this; he wanted to play with the geese but did not want to risk another soaking. One of the geese dipped her head under the water and came up right next to William.

"Come and have some fun," she said as her head appeared next to William. William stepped back; he did not know if she was friendly or threatening. He splashed the water with his paw to try and get back at the goose. Suddenly a dark shadow appeared as a cloud blocked out the sun.

"Uh oh." William knew this feeling; there was something behind him and he did not want to turn around. Jimmy appeared in view, his body was down as he stalked around the corner. His eyes danced with wicked satisfaction.

"Gertrude!" exclaimed one of the other geese, "They're friendly!" She was trying to protect the dogs from the angry goose. Gertrude was not in the mood to be persuaded. She did not like visitors and Jimmy had told her how awful these ones were. She hissed then honked loudly. The noise alone was enough to scare William. He didn't move. He was overawed at the sight of the gigantic creature before him. Gertrude spread her wings showing off her huge wingspan. William's heart rate went through the roof. She put her head down and stretched her neck forward so it looked like a slithering, sinister snake. Then she ran at him. Geese normally have an even stride, but Gertrude's stride was uneven, making her look even more menacing. She let out a blood-curdling honk.

*"I am Gertrude the galloping goose,
And I don't like strangers on my farm.
I have never made a truce,
So beware you may come to harm."*

He knew he had to get out of there, so he was running for his life, again. He was in such a complete state of panic, you could see the whites of his eyes. Gertrude was in flight, her long graceful legs floating beneath her, the sound of her wings beating was reverberating in his ears. She dived at him, grabbing hold of his fur with her beak. William screamed, the sharp pain searing through his body, he turned his head and snapped at her hoping to make her let go. She did and flew up in the air, then charged at him again, flapping her wings furiously. They thudded on the side of William's body sending him tumbling along the field. The fall disoriented him, he stood up and shook trying to regain his focus but that moment of stillness allowed Gertrude a clear aim and she landed on his back. She drummed her huge webbed feet on his back and opened her beak wide, twisted her neck and snapped it shut on the back of his. He howled, the weight of her on his back felt like lead and he was pushed to the floor. He went down thumping the ground with his side, but this allowed him to turn his neck. He bared his teeth and snarled, managing to bite her neck. It didn't break the skin but it was enough to make Gertrude recoil and release him. He took that opportunity to leap forward and run as fast as he could again, frantically trying to escape the clutches of this fiendish goose. In his panic, William didn't see the rabbit hole and he caught his foot in it causing him to dive head first into the ground. The speed carried him into a roll and he groaned as the wind was knocked out of him. He lay panting rapidly, his mouth open wide as he was gasping for air. He was consumed with fear. The terrifying sound of the beating wings had stopped and now there was nothing but an eerie silence. William tensed; he was anticipating something awful was going to happen. He was right. Jimmy appeared in front of him. William stepped back but he had nowhere to go. He gulped.

"Thank you, Gertrude, that's enough now," Jimmy said with a calm voice. Gertrude had petrified William and chased him so far that he was now completely on his own with the awaiting Jimmy.

"How does it feel being that scared?" asked Jimmy, his vivid eyes narrowed and penetrated William. William couldn't look at him, he just wanted him to go away.

"Well," persisted Jimmy, "How does it feel?" His voice was impatient.

"Hideous," William said quietly. He struggled to speak and cut a pathetic figure in front of the ominous Jimmy.

"Now you know how all those poor animals felt when you scared them," Jimmy sneered. William felt helpless. He knew Jimmy was right.

"I'm sorry, I really didn't mean to scare them," William grovelled. He didn't know how to make Jimmy believe him. He shuffled uncomfortably and stared longingly down the field to safety. He had been a fool to leave the protection of Molly. Jimmy was now looking at a pitiful sight and something inside him softened. He had done to William the exact thing that he was angry at William for in the first place and retribution didn't feel as satisfying as he thought it would.

"Come on, I'll take you back," Jimmy's voice had changed, it was now more soothing. William didn't know how to respond; was this a trick? But Jimmy started to walk back in the direction of the farmhouse.

"Are you coming then?" Jimmy called back. William tensed the muscles in his face, he was a little confused, he absolutely thought that he was going to be in serious trouble.

"Y-yes," William stuttered and jumped up, he did not want to be left up here alone. He looked round in trepidation. A loud honk gave him a fright and he flinched.

"Go back, Gertrude, we're done here," Jimmy ordered. Gertrude flapped her wings and flew across the field. As William watched the sinister shadow get smaller and smaller, he could feel his heart rate decreasing.

"I think we need to make a detour first," Jimmy said to William. William's breathing quickened again, had he been wrong to trust Jimmy? Was this just part of a conniving plan to get rid of William once and for all? But William had little choice other than to go with him, so he obediently followed Jimmy with a sense of wariness. Jimmy took William to the sheep field. Panic immediately set in and the sheep started bleating frantically.

"What is he doing here?" snapped an angry ewe.

"He's got something that he wants to say," Jimmy explained. "Let him speak." The bleating abated.

"I am so, so sorry that I scared you," William fawned. "I really never meant to, I just wanted to play and have fun, but I realise now that my behaviour was wrong and I feel very ashamed of what I have done."

"How would you like it if somebody chased you like that?" questioned the angry ewe.

"I wouldn't, not at all," William confessed. He glanced at Jimmy who remained expressionless.

"Make sure you think before you act from now on," the ewe said, appearing not to be that forgiving.

"I will, I promise," William said genuinely.

"Right, well now that's done let's go and find your sister." They went back to the geese where Sam had been waiting nervously.

"William," she was thrilled to see him. "When Gertrude came back without you and said she had left you with Jimmy I didn't think that I would see you again!"

"We had something to sort out," Jimmy uttered, slightly wounded that Sam thought he could have hurt him. He wasn't a malicious dog.

Molly came round the corner, slightly taken aback to see the dogs sitting contentedly together.

"Come on you two, look at the mess you're in," Molly said to William and Sam. "You're going to get me told off by your mum." They said goodbye to the geese and walked out of the field. They both shook vigorously to get rid of as much of the water and debris as they could. As they went back to the farmhouse, Mum, Dad, Lewis and Millie were talking to Fred about the day's events.

"Look at the state of you two," Mum rolled her eyes as they appeared at the farmhouse.

"They were in with the geese having lots of fun," Molly told them, unaware of the terrifying experiences that Jimmy and Gertrude had put William through.

They said their goodbyes; the family thanked Fred and Molly for a lovely day and said how much they had enjoyed themselves. Dad had brought some spare towels to lay in the boot in case the dogs got messy. He covered the boot, picked up the dogs and placed them on the towels. As they drove out of the farm gates, Molly called after them.

"Thanks for all your help, come back any time, all of you." William shot a glance at Sam; he wasn't sure if coming back was a good idea.

Chapter Nine

The children were tired and wanted to get home. Although the car journey was only half an hour, it felt longer than one of Mrs Johnson's maths lessons. Mum laughed,

"Hard work being a farmer, isn't it?"

When they arrived home, Mum picked the dogs up and carried them to the bathroom. William squirmed frantically, he knew what was coming and really did not want a bath.

"Come on, William, it's not that bad," she tried to reassure him and put him in the bath ready for a good scrub. Dad swiftly put Sam in there too.

"Ugh, I hate this," William whinged. Luckily, it does not happen too often as bathing a dog too frequently can destroy the natural oils in their coats. Once the pain of the bath was over, Mum rubbed them down with towels.

"I like this bit," William wriggled in the towel, helping Mum to dry him off. As soon as the bathroom door was opened they both tore down the stairs; a bath always made them go a little crazy. They both lunged onto the mat in the living room and nestled into it trying to dry themselves even more. They did not stay there for long though as they heard their biscuits tumbling into their bowls in the kitchen. They jumped up enthusiastically and buried their heads in their bowls and gobbled up their dinner. Even though they had had an extra meal at lunchtime, William and Sam had worked up a big appetite owing to all the playing and stress of the afternoon. Once they had finished, they went back to the mat where they snuggled in and curled up. William decided that maybe he couldn't be a farm dog after all, besides, life with the family was good.

As William drifted off to sleep,
He thought about the events of the day.
How he had scared the chicken and sheep,
He felt a huge sense of dismay.
Although he never meant to give them a scare,
The moral of the story is . . .
How to approach each animal, you must be aware,
To stop them from getting in a tizz.

THE END